luto ▲▲ Plays

Female Parts

One Woman Plays

by **Dario Fo** and **Franca Rame**
adapted by **Olwen Wymark**

Waking Up
A Woman Alone
The Same Old Story
translated by **Margaret Kunzle**

Medea
translated by **Stuart Hood**

This adaptation first published 1981 by
Pluto Press Limited, Unit 10 Spencer Court,
7 Chalcot Road, London NW1 8LH

ISBN 0 86104 220 4

Cover photo by Mario Falsaperla, Milan
Cover design by Michael Mayhew

Typeset by Malvern Printers, Malvern
Printed in Great Britain by Spider Web Offset,
London NW3

Pluto Press will be publishing in English the work of
Dario Fo and Franca Rame. *Accidental Death of an
Anarchist* and *We Can't Pay, We Won't Pay!* are
already in print. Dario Fo's *Mistero Buffo* will be
published autumn 1981.

Introduction

The plays in this volume are the result of a close collaboration between Franca Rame and Dario Fo. Together they represent a tradition of writing and performance which has its roots in the ancient popular theatre of Italy—a tradition which they have made the basis for a highly successful political theatre.

Franca Rame belongs to a family of travelling players which even under fascism performed in the small towns and villages of Italy. It was in this hard school that she learnt the art of improvisation (at which she excels) of working with a minimum of sets and props, and of making a major contribution to a company in which everyone shares in the organisation of a performance.

Dario Fo came to the theatre from stage design but soon developed an extraordinary talent as a comic actor and as a writer. In both these capacities he draws on the tradition of the *commedia dell'arte*, that brilliant improvisatory tradition which came to France from Italy, which influenced Molière, and left its mark in a somewhat degenerate form in British pantomime.

From the time of their marriage in 1954, Franca Rame and Dario Fo have worked closely together in 'bourgeois comedies', on television and in political theatre, at times playing before huge audiences in factories, on parking lots and in circus tents. Their decisive commitment to political theatre came in 1968 when, as Fo has said, he decided to stop being the 'jester of the bourgeoisie' and with Franca Rame resolved to use their talents towards the struggle for radical change in Italian society. At first they worked under the auspices of the Italian Communist Party, but their satirical criticism of the party line, of party bureaucracy and of revisionism led to a break in 1970 and the setting up of their own political collective 'La Comune', with its headquarters in Milan.

It was inevitable that Dario Fo and Franca Rame should become the subject of attack and censorship. When they appeared in the popular Italian television series *Canzonissima*, their sketches were censored for their iv

political content. The Italian Communist Party has continued to boycott their plays. A television performance of Dario Fo's *Mistero Buffo*, based on medieval mystery plays with a strong anti-clerical thrust, led to bitter attacks from the clergy and the Christian Democrats. Only after sharp political struggle was La Comune able to retain their Milan headquarters where the company had been based for many years. In Sardinia, Fo was arrested and imprisoned for alleged violations of theatre agreements and in the same year—1973—a fascist group abducted Franca Rame and beat her up. The intervention of La Comune in Italian politics, witness *Accidental Death of an Anarchist*, is direct and powerful.

The works performed by Franca Rame and Dario Fo and the result of close collaboration between them are comedies but comedies which deal with situations both unbearable and unbearably tragic. The tension at the heart of their performances lies in the tug between the grimness of the situation portrayed and the grotesque behaviour of the protagonists— especially of bureaucrats, the police, the judiciary and, in the case of these plays, of men. In performance there is produced in the audience a kind of astonishment which finds its expression in laughter but behind which there is the shock of recognition: this is how women are,

in our society this is how they are treated.

These four monologues are a direct political intervention by Franca Rame in a society where the role of women is notably restricted by the Church, by the state and by male society. But they have a reference beyond Italy, demonstrated by the success with which they have been performed all over Europe.

Waking Up is about the double exploitation of woman as worker and housewife. *A Woman Alone* shows woman as prisoner of her husband, and as sex object. *The Same Old Story* is about sexual repression and a woman's rebellion. The last play, *Medea*, sees children as a yoke hung by society on the necks of women to make them 'easier to milk and easier to mount'. Her sacrifice of her children allows a new woman to be born.

Franca Rame and Dario Fo work within a tradition of improvisation which means the texts of their plays are difficult to 'fix'; they change according to the changing political situation, according to the different audiences. They are like living organisms but within them there is a hard skeletal framework—framework of radical criticism of our society and of relationships within it.

Stuart Hood

Female Parts: One-Woman Plays

by Dario Fo and Franca Rame

Adapted by Olwen Wymark

These plays were first performed in
English at the National Theatre,
London on 26 June 1981.

Yvonne Bryceland plays the only role
in each play.

Director: Michael Bogdanov
Designers: Sue Jenkinson and
            John Bury

Waking Up

Onstage a double bed, bedside table with lamp and clock on it, cupboard, sideboard, table, washing machine, gas cooker, fridge, sink and a cot with a baby (doll) in it.

In the bed a man and woman sleeping. The woman is having a nightmare and making wild gestures with her arms.

(Muttering) Weld. Drill. Two rivets. Cut. *(Louder)* Weld. Drill. Two rivets. Cut. *(Getting louder and louder)* Weld. Drill. Two rivets. Cut. Weld! Drill! Two rivets! Cut. *(Screams)* Oh my God I've cut off all my fingers! Quick ... pick them up, pick them up, don't leave them lying around. The boss likes everything neat and tidy. Pick up those fingers before he comes, quick!

She sits up with a jolt, her eyes still closed. Holds her hands out in front of herself and wails

My fingers, oh my poor fingers! I'll never be able to pick my nose again! *(Opens her eyes. Joy and relief)* They're still here! I've got

them! Hello fingers. *(She kisses them. Then she yawns and groans)* Now I even dream about the bloody factory. Isn't working there enough? *(Then anxious)* What time is it? *(Switches on the lamp and picks up the clock)* Half past six! You didn't go off, you bastard!

She slams the clock down on the table and scrambles out of bed putting on her dressing gown and slippers.

Half past six ... oh God I'll be late. Bloody thing, why didn't it go off? *(Runs to the cot)* Come on baby, time to start the day. Wake up Mama's honeybun. Time to get up! *(Picks baby up)* Up up up and away!

She swoops the doll over to the table making zooming airplane noise. Breaks off abruptly in mid zoom.

You're wet! Oh you little pisspot and I'm in such a hurry! How can you be wet again? I got up and changed you three hours ago. *(Puts baby on table. Laughs at him as she takes off its nappy)* You're just a pissy

pissy baby yes you are yes you are yes you are. *(Then with mock severity)* We have to rush! You know perfectly well if we get to the nursery one teeny tiny minute after seven o'clock the nuns will just send us right back home again. Come on now, Mama's going to wash your botty-bum.

Takes the baby to the sink and turns on the tap.

Just a little bit of hot water and we'll ... no bloody hot water! I bet that daft Luigi let the boiler go out. No he's not daft, it's coming hot now. *(Washes the baby)* And now we'll wash baby's little facey ... shh shh don't cry, you'll wake up Daddy. *(She takes the baby back to the table)* Lucky Daddy's got another half hour to sleep before he has to zap out into the world and do his Tarzan bit. *(She gives the Tarzan call)* Aaaaaeeeeeaaaaaeeeaaa! *(Realises she's been too loud and puts her hand over her mouth glancing over at the bed. Then sotto voce)* Aaaaaaeeeeeaaaeeeaaaa!

Then miming the following with exaggerated movements

Off to the factory, run for the bus, get to the station, jump on the train and then! Luigi! The performing chimpanzee on the assembly line! Reach up. Push down. Step on the pedal. Reach up. Push down. Step on the pedal. Reach up ... *(Laughs)* That's right! Laugh at your mama. You like to watch me make a monkey out of

myself don't you. Now before we put on your nice clean nappy we'll give you a lovely sprinkle of *(Reaches for jar and sprinkles baby's bottom)* grated cheese? Who put grated cheese in here instead of talcum powder? Woops ... what a mess! Never mind, never mind, we'll just pop it back into the jar.

Brushes grated cheese off the baby and puts cheese back in jar.

Can't afford to waste good cheese nowadays can we? I'll put it in the minestrone tonight. *(Then putting nappy on baby)* Anyway, my baby's got the cleanest little bottybum in the world don't you, eh? *(Then urgent again)* Quick, quick we mustn't be late my little pisserino. Lie there while Mama washes her face.

Rushes to the sink and washes her face and hands while singing.

"You'll be a little lovelier each day with fabulous pink Camay. You'll be a little ..." Oh bloody hell the water's stopped, there's no more water! Mad! Three hundred families in this building and every single one of them wants to get washed the same minute as me! How am I going to rinse off this fabulous pink creamy lather eh? Ouch! It's in my eyes!

She grabs a towel and wipes the soap off her face.

Oh well who cares? I'll wash later. Nobody's going to look at me anyway. Ah, but they might sniff me. *(Gets deodorant aerosol)* Modern science and its wonders! A little spray every day takes the B.O. away! *(Sprays armpit. Screams)* What did I do? It burns! *(Reads from can)* 'Handy Spray-on Radiator Paint'. Oh my God I've got a silver armpit! How am I going to get it off? *(Starts pulling on her clothes)* I know, I know ... I'll use some of that solvent at the factory. *(Dashes over to the clock)* What's the time now? Six forty. I think we'll make it, baby!

Rushing round the room she picks up her things and the baby

Mama's jacket, Mama's handbag, Mama's baby, Mama's key ...

She's heading for the door. She stops dead.

Where's Mama's key?

She puts down the baby and goes through all her pockets.

It's gone. It's gone. Where did I put it? *(Dashes around looking)* Where is it? Where is it? Oh this is so typical! Every second counts and I can't find my bloody key. I can't stand it. I'll go out of my mind!

Stands still and takes a deep breath.

All right, now just take it easy. What exactly did I do when I came in last night? We'll go through every single thing step by step. Reconstruction! Right. When I got home Luigi wasn't back yet so I had to unlock the door.

Picks up the baby and acts the following.

Mama's baby under the right arm, Mama's bag over the left arm ... and ... Mama's key in the left hand. I put the bag down here, and I put the baby in his cot and then I went straight out the door again to get the shopping bag.

Goes to the door and mimes picking up shopping. Looks at her hand.

Key still in my hand? Yep. And a carton of milk under my arm. I come back in, I put the shopping bag down on the table and I put the milk in the fridge. *(Stops as she approaches fridge)* Oh hey! I bet I put the key in the fridge too. I am mad! I'll kill myself!

Opens refrigerator door.

Not in the butter dish, not in the egg compartment, not in the ice cube tray ... no, didn't put the key in the fridge. *(Pause)* Didn't put the milk in either. *(Takes plastic carton out of fridge)* But I did put the lemon flavoured washing up liquid in. Well, lemons belong in the fridge don't they? I am definitely losing my mind. So where did I put the milk? In the washing machine? *(Looks)* No. Well that's a relief ... but where? Wait, I've got it! I put the milk down by the cooker so I could do the baby's bottle. Then I had to have both my hands free to open the milk carton so ... I put the key between my teeth. *(Mimes this. Then speaks through clenched teeth)* Why in my teeth? Why not on the table? *(Then shrugs as she mimes pouring milk into saucepan)* Who knows? Okay the baby's milk is on the stove. I light the baby ... I mean I light the milk ... oh I mean I light the gas! And then I go and peel the baby ... I mean peel his clothes off for his bath.

She mimes picking up the baby.

I put the baby down on the table and ... no wait a minute the milk's boiling over! *(Dashes to cooker miming holding the baby still)* I turn off the gas and I carry the baby over to the cupboard and get his bath out.

She mimes taking bath out of cupboard with both hands.

(Through clenched teeth again) Still got the key between my teeth! I put the bathtub down on the table and then I ... *(Looks wildly round)* Where's the baby! He's gone! I've lost my baby! Where did I put him? In the fridge? In the washing machine? In the cupboard? *(Mimes taking baby out of cupboard. Kisses it)* Oh my poor little baby. I was so upset I had to get a drink of water. *(Gulps)* Oh my God I bet I swallowed the key! No I couldn't've. The key's got a hole in it. Luigi would've been nagging me all night about whistling in bed. *(Desperate)* Where did I put that key? Where? Where? Calm down. Just calm down. The next thing I did was *(Miming)* fill the tub with

hot water and then I got the jar of bicarbonate of soda. *(Gets a jar of the shelf)* I always put two spoonfuls of bicarb in his bath to make the water soft. Oh yes, the water here is ... *(Breaks off. Stares into jar)* Hey? What's this. Sugar? Who put sugar in the soda jar? *(Gets another jar down and opens it)* Woops ... and soda in the sugar jar! Since when have I been bathing my baby in sugar water? Oh ... so that's why that nun said she couldn't ever put him out in the playground. "The minute I put him outside all the bees and wasps and flies start buzzing around him," she said. Poor little thing. Oh ... and poor old Luigi. No wonder he's been burping all the way through breakfast lately. I've been putting soda in his coffee! *(Laughs but then agitated again)* But where's my key? If I don't find it I'll ... wait a minute I've got it! What an idiot I am. Now I remember. I never even took it out of the door! While I was bathing the baby I heard Luigi scraping and scratching away with his key and swearing like mad because when I came in I locked the door behind me and left my key inside the lock!

Miming the following

So I picked up the baby and I went and unlocked the door to let Luigi in. Screaming blue murder by that time he was. I know I had the key in my hand then because I waved it under his nose and I said "Okay okay! I left my key in the lock.

Why don't you kill me? Go on, kill me, kill your wife, get your name in the papers!" "Leave off," he says, "It isn't you ... it's that fucking train. An hour late! Would you believe a train could take an hour and a half to do twelve miles? And that's just time down the drain you know. Nobody pays me for it. Do you think the boss gives a damn about all the hours I spend getting out to his bloody factory just so I can bloody work for him?" "Well don't take it out on me," I said. *(Looks down at her hand)* Still with the key in my hand? Yes, still there. "Anyway they don't call them bosses anymore," I said. "They're multi-nationals now. Only dogs have bosses. We're free people now ... liberated, didn't you know? Listen Luigi," I said, "You get mad about how nobody pays you for your travelling time but what about me? Do I get paid for all the working and slaving I do at home? No I do not. And believe you me everything I do here is *for* the multinational, oh yes!" And then I went to get the baby's milk.

Goes to the cot and mimes putting the baby in.

I put him in his cot while I went to fix the bottle. *(Heads for the cooker. Doubles back)* Wait a minute ... did the key fall into the cot then? *(Bends over the cot)* No it isn't there. *(Suddenly freezes. In mild tones)* I don't believe it. *(Then with passion)* You stinker! How

could you do this to me?

Picks up the baby and carries him to the table.

If I've told you once I've told you a hundred times ... wait till you get to the nursery! Do your poo *after* seven o'clock and then the nuns have to change you. We haven't got time for this now ... we're going to be late! Look at the time ... I'm never going to make it. *(Momentarily very upset)* I'll lose a day's pay! *(And then as she is taking off the baby's nappy suddenly laughs)* How could all this lot come out of one teeny tiny little bum? King Poo you are!

She carries the baby to the sink and once again washes its bottom.

"Oh yes, Luigi," I said. "They invented the family and they called it sacred just to keep all you nervous wrecks on the assembly line from going completely bonkers. You come home from the factory to an all-purpose unpaid wife that you can take it out on like a spare mattress. We recondition you, regenerate you ... reproduce you! And all for free! We feed you, we wash you, we dress you and brush you down and send you back to the factory as good as new and for what? So you can work even harder for the multi-national, that's for what! He's like God Almighty, that multinational. He makes the boom and he makes the crash, he makes depression, inflation, the galloping economic crisis, the slow creeping economic crisis, the falling lire, the eurodollar, the petrodollar ... he makes it all! But he just shrugs his shoulders and he says, 'Nothing I can do about it. It's just the way things go.'"

She starts putting on the baby's clean nappy.

Then Luigi gives this really irritating little laugh. "Oh ho!" he says. "I didn't know I was married to a radical. Get Mrs Women's Lib! Since when have you been listening to the feminists?"

She mimes turning on him in a rage.

"Listen, Stupid," I tell him, "I don't need to listen to feminists or radicals or anybody else to find out what a shitty life we lead. We both work like dogs and we never have a minute to talk. We never talk to each other! Is that marriage? Like does it ever even enter your mind to think about what's going on inside me? How I feel? Ever ask me if I'm tired ... if you could give me a hand? Ha!"

Mimes bearing down on him threateningly.

"Who does the cooking? Me! Who does the washing up? Me! Who does the shopping? Me! And who does the death-defying financial acrobatics so we can get through to the end of the month? Me me me! And I'm working full time at the factory, remember. Your dirty socks ... who washes them eh? How many times have you washed my socks? We should talk to each other, Luigi! We never talk. I mean it's okay with me that your problems are my problems but why can't my problems be your problems too instead of yours being ours and mine being only mine. I want us to live together ... not just in the same place. We should talk to each other! But what do we do? You come home from work, watch the telly and go to bed. Day after day it's always the same. Oh, except for Sundays. *(Scornfully)* Hooray hooray it's football day! Every Sunday off you go to watch twenty two idiots in their underpants kicking a ball around and some other mentally deficient maniac dashing up and down blowing a whistle!" He ... that Luigi ... he went purple in the face! You'd think I'd insulted his mother. "How could a person like *you* ever know the first thing about sport?" *(Brief pause)* Not the best thing he could've said, really *(With relish)* I freaked. "Who the fuck would want to?" I shouted at him. And then I really started raving on like a lunatic. Oh I said it all. Everything! I screamed at him, he yelled back at me, I screamed louder, he yelled louder ... we were just about shouting the building down. So finally I said "Right! If this is marriage we've made a mistake!" And I picked up my mistake and I walked out.

*She picks up the baby and starts
for the door. Stops, thoughtful.*

I definitely had the key then because
I opened the door with it. *(Heads
for the door again. Stops)* Luigi
came over and grabbed hold of me.
He was white as a sheet, poor
thing. I'd never said all that stuff
before and I think it really got to
him. "Don't be like that," he says
and he pulls me back into the
room. "We will talk," he says.
"We'll talk right now. Then if you
still want to leave me okay but first
we have to talk. It's a question of
dialectics," he says. "what we need
here is a calm, rational
discussion." So he pulls me down
on the bed.

*She sits on the bed, lays the baby
down and approvingly pats the
sleeping Luigi.*

He said I was in the right and he was
in the wrong. He said everything I
said was true and he was entirely to
blame. He said the thing was he
was used to his mother waiting on
him all the time and he thought I
was like that too. He said yes it
was all his fault and yes he realised
all his mistakes and he said why
didn't I say anything like this
before and he said definitely he
would change.

*Strokes Luigi affectionately and
laughs.*

He had a real Self-Criticism session
and he was so good at it it made
me cry. The more he criticised

himself the more I cried and the
more I cried the more he criticised
himself. *(Luxuriously)* Oh I had a
really fantastic cry last night!

Suddenly galvanised, she jumps up.

But what about the key? *(Closes her
eyes and speaks concentratedly)*
Luigi took it out of my hand and
then he ... *(Opens eyes. Fast)* put it
in his pocket!

*Runs over to Luigi's jacket which
is hanging up. Looks in pocket.*

Eureka!

*Holds up the key triumphantly.
Sudden anxiety again.*

What time is it?

Rushes over and looks at the clock.

Ten to seven ... we can still make it.
Come on, honeybun, let's go!
(Grabbing her things) Baby, jacket,
bag, key ... and we're off!

Heads for the door. Stops.

Hang on. Season ticket. *(Puts baby
on table)* Better get it out now, eh?
Then I won't have to put you down
on the floor of the bus and have
people stepping all over you.

*Rummages in bag. Finds ticket,
takes it out, picks up baby.*

Here we are ... Mama's weekly
season ticket. See? *(Shows it to the
baby)* Okay, now we're all ready to
... *(Breaks off. Stares at ticket)*
Hey? What's this? Six punches? Six
punches going and six punches
return? Who made all these holes

in my ticket? *(Baffled)* Six holes ... it doesn't make sense. It just ... *(Then stares at the baby)* What day is it?

Goes over to calendar hanging on wall and looks at it. Pause. Speaks almost in a whisper.

Sunday.

Shouts.

Sunday!

(To the baby) And you never said a word!

Dances around the room with the baby.

It's Sunday. I'm out of my mind. I wanted to go to work on Sunday! I'm a raving nut! It's Sunday! *(Singing it)* Sunday's not a work day, Sunday is a sleep day, back to bed my baby, back to bed!

She sits down on the bed and hugs the baby

I'm going to dream a beautiful dream about a world where every single day is Sunday. A lifetime of Sundays. Sunday forever. Sunday rules okay? They've hanged Monday, they've shot Tuesday and oh what they didn't do to poor old Friday. Back to bed, baby, we get to sleep! And if I dream about working again I'll strangle myself! *(And as she lies down on the bed and pulls the blankets up covering herself and the baby completely)* Sleep! Sleep! Sleep!

End of play

A Woman Alone

Lights up on a woman downstage centre, ironing. She's in her early thirties dressed in a more or less see-through negligée and high heeled slippers. A portable radio is playing pop music very loud. There are five doors leading off. She plays throughout as if facing a window which is only a few feet away from the window of the flat opposite. Bored and expressionless, she irons in rhythm to the music, executing sketchy dance steps. At one point she raises her arms and, with the iron in one hand, moves her arms to the music. Suddenly her face lights up with surprise and pleasure. She comes further downstage.

Hey! Hey Signora, good morning! *(Louder)* I said good morning. How long have you been living over there? *(Shouts)* I said how long ago did you move in? I thought that apartment was still empty. I'm so glad somebody's moved in. What? *(Even louder)* I said I'm glad! I'm glad! What's the matter, can't you hear me? What? The what? Oh yes. Right. Wait.

She runs over to the radio and turns it off and goes back to window.

Sorry. When I'm on my own I always have the radio on. If it isn't turned up full blast I get this feeling I might hang myself. I've got the stereo on in the living room. Listen.

Goes to living room door and opens it. Blast of classical music. The music cuts off as she shuts the door.

Did you hear it? And the cassette player's going in the kitchen.

Goes to kitchen door, opens it, blast of jazz, closes it.

See? Whatever room I go into I've got company. What? *(Shocked)* Oh not the bedroom, of course no! My goodness no. I've got the television on in there.

Goes to bedroom door. Opens it. Blast of plain chant.

(Shouts) Oh yes I always keep it pretty loud. That's a high mass! In Polish *(Music cuts off as she shuts the door)* Polish ... what a daft

language, eh? You can't understand a word of it. Just right for a pope!

She goes back to her ironing.

Oh yes I like Church music too even though it's really hopeless to dance to. Any kind of music really, as long as it's loud. It keeps me company, you see. How do you keep yourself company, Signora? Ahhh ... a child! Aren't you lucky!

Pause. Looks at the small jacket she's been pressing.

How silly I am. I've got a child myself. Two! A big one and a little one.

Brings the jacket further downstage, sits and brushes it.

No no, they don't keep me company, oh no. The big one's started school and she's got her own friends. The little boy's at home the whole time but he's no company either. He's too young. He's a baby ... even though he snores like an old man. Sleep? Sleeps all the time! *(Sighs)* If only he'd grow up. *(Then hastily bright)* But I'm not complaining. I love it at home. I've got everything. My husband gives me everything I need. Like ... like I've got ... *(Looks round)* ... I've got a refrigerator! What? Well yes I know everybody has refrigerators but mine *(Impressive)* makes round ice cubes. *(Serious again)* And I've got a washing machine with twenty four different programs. There's

one that's for such delicate things I could wash paper in it ... I could! Trouble is I never have any paper to wash. And a dryer too. You would not believe how dry this dryer dries. Amazing. Sometimes I have to get all the clothes wet again ... they're too dry to iron.

Reminded, she goes back to the iron. Lays a shirt out on the board.

Oh and a cleaning lady. Oh yes ... I used to have a cleaning lady working for me. But she left. Then another one came. But she left too. They all leave. They just can't stand it in my house. No no, not because of me. My brother in law. He touches them all. If they get anywhere near him ... grab! You know. Right there. He's not well, poor boy. What? Perverted? Oh I don't know about that. All I know is that he wanted to do things and they wouldn't let him. Quite right too, really. Well imagine it. There you are busy busy doing the housework and all of a sudden this hand comes up at you from underneath. Grab! And what a hand he's got ... you should see it. Just as well he's only got the one.

Brings the shirt downstage and sits again as she sews on a button.

No no, an accident. A car crash. Terrible. He was all smashed up and him only thirty. They put him in a plaster cast from head to foot. Only a little hole here for breathing and eating. He can't really talk through it ... *(Mumbles)* just mumbles like this. Oh and his eyes aren't covered. They were okay. Lovely big eyes he's got ... always staring at you. And they left out this hand of his too because it was just about the only part of him that wasn't broken. Well ... *(Embarrassed)* there is another part of him that wasn't smashed either. What? Well it's ... I don't know how to say it, Signora. We've known each other such a short time, I wouldn't like you to get a bad impression. Let's say he's quite ... sound *(Then doing an exaggerated pelvic thrust)* there! *(Rueful)* And how sound! Too sound. He never stops wanting to ... well you know. Hmmm? Oh yes yes he does think about other things. He reads a lot, you know. To educate himself. Reads all the time. *(Pause)* Pornography. His room is full of filthy magazines ... those ones with naked women in ... certain positions? Uncomfortable! I bet some of them need a plaster cast like my brother in law after all that. Disgusting ... all those parts of anatomy blown up in full colour. Do you know it can take me fully fifteen minutes to figure out what part I'm looking at?

Folds up shirt and goes back to the ironing.

Since all the cleaning ladies left I have to look after my brother in law myself. I do it for my husband's sake. *(Indignant)* What, me? What an idea! Certainly not. With me he's different. He respects me. He's very polite ... he always asks my permission before he grabs.

Telephone rings

Oh that's my husband. He always rings me up about now. Excuse me a minute. *(Picks up phone. Sweetly)* Hello. *(Pause)* What? *(Pause)* Fuck off you bastard! *(Slams down the phone. To woman opposite)* I do beg your pardon. I never swear but when you must you must, mustn't you. What? No that wasn't my husband ... I don't know who it was. He's a heavy breather that talks. A real pig! He rings me up two or three ... or four thousand times a day and says filthy things to me. Some of the words he uses aren't even in the dictionary. I know ... I looked. Yes of course that kind of person is sick, I know! Listen I've already got one sick man here. I can't take care of all the dirty old men in Italy!

Telephone rings

There he goes again. I'll show him! *(Picks up phone. Hard and fast)* Listen, pig, this telephone is being tapped by the police so you'd better just ... oh. *(Then with enthusiastic affection)* Hello! *(Covers phone. To woman opposite)* It's my husband! *(Back to phone)* No of course not, Aldo dear, I didn't mean you. I thought you were somebody else. Who? Oh. A ... a man who keeps on telephoning and ... uh ... asking for you! He sounds furious and his language is terrible! What? Well he says ... uh ... he says you owe him a lot of money! Yes! So I thought I'd frighten him by mentioning the police you see. No, he's never said what his name was. Why? Is there somebody you ... What? *(Outraged)* What are you talking about? I'm at home! Aldo I swear I'm at home. What number did you dial just now eh? Right! And who answered it? So where else can I be? Have I been out? You are asking me if I've been ... you'll drive me round the bend! How could I *get* out? *(To woman opposite)* Oh Signora, my husband is so ... *(Back to phone)* What? No there isn't anybody here. Just me, all alone. *(Exasperated)* Well when I talk to myself I call myself Signora, all right? Yes your brother's fine. He's in his room looking at his blue movies. Yes the baby's fine too. Yes he woke up and got fed. Yes he did peepee ... yes your brother did too. Don't worry! Who's getting mad? I just said not to worry. Everybody in the house has peed! Goodbye. No, I'm feeling happy, Aldo. I've been here ironing and just laughing and singing away. I'm very happy, Aldo! *(Shouts)* I'm happy!

Hangs up and gives inarticulate bellow of rage at phone. Then comes back down to the window.

You see? I had to lie to him. If I told him the truth about the talking heavy breather on the phone he'd say it was all my own fault. He'd say I must be getting some kind of kick out of talking to a pervert or there wouldn't be any kicks in it for the pervert. He'd probably have the phone cut off. He already keeps me locked in the house. Yes it's true, he really does. Every morning when he goes out he locks me in. The what? Oh he does all the shopping.

She starts ironing again.

How do you mean if there was an emergency? Oh no ... nothing could ever happen in my house. We're such a quiet family. Anyway he always phones me during the day and I ... *(Breaks off. Her tone suddenly icy)* Excuse me.

Her gaze has gone higher and now she shouts

I can see you, you creep, I can see you! Don't try and hide. Your binoculars are shining in the sun!

She covers one of her breasts with a tiny handkerchief she's ironing and puts the iron over the other breast. Screams.

Oh my God I've ironed my breast!

Puts iron down and attempts to cover both breasts with the handkerchief

It's all his fault. No you can't see him, his window's on the floor above you. It's all I need isn't it ... a peeping tom. A poor woman can't even dress in casual clothes to do the ironing in her own home.

Because of him I should do the housework in my overcoat. *(Shouting at peeping tom)* Right? With a balaclava and ski boots eh? *(Then tragically to woman opposite)* And I don't even know how to ski. I'd probably end up in a plaster cast like my brother in law. What? No I'm not calling the police thanks very much. I can just imagine them and their questions. *(Official voice)* What was I wearing on the day in question. To what degree might I have been described to be ... unclothed. Is it not a fact that I was being deliberately provocative. *(Own voice)* Oh yes. What do you want to bet I'd be the one that was charged. With indecent behaviour in domestic premises which were exposed to the view of an innocent member of the public! I don't need the police. Not while I've got this. *(Goes to the back wall and gets a rifle)* I'll take care of him myself. Maybe this will be my lucky day.

Crouched over she comes stealthily back to the window. Stands up, points rifle and shouts

I'll kill you!

Disappointed, she lowers the gun.

Escaped again. Just one peep at this and that's him gone every time. *(Shouts)* Coward! Creep! Dirty snooper! *(Pretends to shoot)* Bang bang! Bang!

Puts the gun down, looks at woman opposite and laughs

I suppose it is quite funny, really. Bet you think I'm a nutcase. *(Starts ironing again)* Well, better a bit bonkers than the way I was before. Every few months I'd get so desperate I'd start swallowing pills. Sleeping pills, aspirins, tranquillisers, antihistamine ... everything I could lay my hands on. Even the kids' castor oil. Anything to kill me ... anything just to die. *(Importantly)* Once I slashed my wrists. Yes. Three months ago. See? I've still got the scars. *(Pause)* Oh no, Signora, please don't ask me to tell you the story about that. No I'm sorry, it's just too intimate and private. It wouldn't be right. After all, we hardly know each other. *(Pause)* Shall I tell you? *(Very brief pause)* Yes I will. I don't know ... I've got a real feeling of *(Searching for the word)* empathy for your building since you moved in. I will tell you. It might do me good ... get it out of my system. Oh it's such a sad story, Signora! It was all because of this boy. *(Tenderly)* Fifteen years younger than me and he looked even younger than that. So sweet, so sensitive, so delicate and shy. Even to imagine making love with this boy would have been a terrible thing. Oh terrible. Like ... like incest. Yes, incest! *(Brief pause)* I did it. *(Surprised)* Did what? The incest. I made love with this boy and the most awful thing was I wasn't even ashamed. I was happy! I sang all day long. But at night I'd cry in bed. *(Dramatic *relish)* "You're depraved!"

Sound of honking from offstage

Oh excuse me a moment. That's my brother in law sounding his horn for me. Be right back.

Goes to another door and sticks her head round it.

What is it dear? No not now. No, I'm talking to a friend.

Shuts door. Telephone rings. She answers it.

Hello? What is it, Aldo? What? If he comes ... if who comes? The man about the money? *(Baffled)* On the telephone? What man? Oh! Oh that man on the telephone! Oh yes. Well what if he does? I'm locked in aren't I. I can't very well invite him in through the keyhole. Oh I see ... pretend I'm not at home. Yes. Yes. Yes. *(Nodding)* Turn off the radio, turn off the stereo, turn off the T.V. Right. Absolutely. Everything off. Yes sir! *(Warm)* Listen I'll do even more for you. *(Malevolent)* I'll go into the bathroom, dive into the toilet and pull the chain! *(Pause)* What? Oh terrific, you're mad now are you? Well why don't you just go to hell!

Hangs up, turns to woman opposite. Forced laugh.

He says when he gets home he'll smash my face in. Who, my husband? *(Incredulous)* Hit *me*? *(Brief pause)* All the time. Sometimes the way he punches me you'd think he was beating up

another man! *(Pause)* Well come to think of it that's one way I do get equal rights.

She goes back to her ironing

But he says he only does it because he loves me so much. *(Fond)* He says I'm still just a baby and he has to protect me. *(Another brief pause)* From everybody but himself! He 'protects' me by locking me up like a battery hen and then he beats me up and then ... he wants to make love! Couldn't care less if I don't feel like it. Always ready, that's me. Instant. Like Nescafe. Washed, brushed, deodorised, shaved legs and armpits ... all smooth and warm and eager. And silent. All I'm supposed to do is just breathe. Oh and give a few little squeals and sighs every now and then so he'll think everything's fine. Well let me tell you everything is far from fine between my husband and me. I don't enjoy it. No, I don't feel anything. With my husband I have never never had a ... had a ... oh that word! What a word, what an awful word! I can't bear to say it even. Orgasm. *(Pause)* Orgasm. It sounds like some kind of hideous creature. Like a cross between an orang outang and a cataclysm. I can just see it in the headlines. *(With flourish)* "Fully Grown Orgasm Escapes from American Circus!" Or "Nun at Zoo Attacked by Crazed Orgasm!" And whenever they talk about "reaching orgasm" all I can see is somebody running like mad to catch a bus!

Looks at woman opposite and laughs

Good. I'm glad you think it's funny too. Orgasm! It's like a bogeyman to frighten the children. Why didn't they use a nice sensible word like ... like chair for instance? You could say *(Does some heavy panting, then in an exhausted voice)* "I reached a chair." Then at least you could rest! *(Pause)* Where was I? All this talking about orgams has made me lose the thread. Oh yes ... my husband. It's true. I don't feel a thing with him. Nothing, no matter how hard I try. Look. I'll show you how I make love with my husband. Like this!

She stands bolt upright, legs apart, arms curved stiffly out in front as though embracing someone, eyes closed. Then opens eyes briefly to look at woman opposite.

Only I'm flat on my back, of course.

Resumes pose, closes eyes again, remains still for a moment then opens eyes

And when he's finished I say "At ease!" *(Takes up soldier's at ease stance)* No, not out loud ... he'd hit me. To myself. Then I relax and go to sleep. *(Shrugs)* Nothing. Every time nothing. Maybe it's because I only ever had one other sexual experience before my husband. No, nothing that time either. He was hopeless! He was twelve ... I was ten. The only thing I felt was a terrible pain ... here. *(Points to her navel)* Well we didn't

know anything about it all, you see, except that babies come out of your stomach so we thought that must be the place for love. *(Points to navel again)* So there he was with his thing ... pushing and pushing. My belly button was all red for days! My mother thought I'd got the measles. But when I grew up and got engaged my girlfriends explained it all to me. *(Rapturous)* On my wedding day I was so excited! In church I was singing to myself *(Sings)* "Love is coming. Love is coming." *(Flat)* But my husband arrived instead. On the wedding night I thought "That's it? Is that all?" Oh I was so disappointed the first time. *(Brief pause)* And the hundredth. And I couldn't talk to anybody about it, you see, I couldn't. Not in those days. But I started reading women's magazines and one day I found out something extraordinary! Listen to this.

Looks carefully round and then comes down to the window. Conspiratorial

We women have got things called Erogenous Zones! *(Nods wisely)* Yes. Now what these are are places *on us* that are very sensitive sexually and they ... what? Oh. *(Disappointed)* You already knew about them. You know a lot don't you. *(Sighs)* Right. *(Then hopeful)* Bet you don't know how many erogenous zones we've got. *(Pleased)* No? Well in this magazine there was a drawing of a naked lady all divided up into sections. You know ... like those posters in the butcher's shop of a cow? And all the erogenous zones were painted these incredible colours. For instance, the rump was painted shocking pink. *(Does a bump and grind and laughs)* Then this part here *(Putting her hands on her back just below her neck)* ... butchers call it chuck. It was purple. And the fillet ... *(Briefly diverted)* What about the price of fillet nowadays eh? Terrible. Well anyway, it was orange. And then the sirloin! *(Pause. Sighs pleasurably)* Ah, the sirloin!

She clasps her hands, closes her eyes, rotates her hips and sings her love is coming tune. Stops. Opens her eyes.

But with my husband? No sirloin, no chuck, no fillet ... no brisket! No nothing. "Well," I thought to myself, "Better just get used to it. That's the way it is for us women." And then I met the boy!

Comes down to the window and sits

The thing was when my little girl got old enough for school I said to my husband "I'm tired of being just a housewife. I want to do something intellectual for a change. I could learn a language, for instance. Maybe English ... because if we ever go to England they talk it like mad over there. All of them ... all the time!" "Why not?" he says, "Good idea." And he brings me home this boy. *(Pause)* Twenty

years old. A drop-out from university. Spoke wonderful English. Well we started our lessons and in no time at all I realised this boy was madly in love with me. Every time I looked at him he'd blush and if I happened to touch his hand he'd start trembling all over and stuttering out the English so you couldn't understand a word. Oh it was all so sensitive and spiritual! Absolutely new to me, Signora. There'd never been anything like that in my life before. All I knew about was my brother in law grabbing me, the heavy breather talking horrible filth at me and my husband *(Pause, looking for word)* functioning with me! So I said to myself "Are you sliding towards sin?" And I gave up English. He took it terribly badly, the boy. Every morning when I went out to shop, there he'd be. Down there in the doorway waiting for me. I didn't want people talking, naturally, so I'd say *(out of the corner of her mouth like a gangster)* "Scram. Get lost. I'm old enough to be your mother. Get a girl your own age, kid. *(Suddenly shouts)* Go away!" Poor thing, he'd get such a shock when I did that. But I can't help it ... when I get excited or upset I just do sort of shout. Then one day when I went out in the morning as usual he wasn't there. Oh I was so disappointed. "Never mind," I thought. "It's all for the best. He's finally given up." And then I saw! The walls of the houses in the street were covered in letters about a foot high in red paint. I LOVE YOU MARIA. That's me, I'm Maria. I LOVE YOU MARIA! In English so nobody could understand it! I ran straight back up the stairs and slammed the door. I turned up the radio as loud as it would go. "No no no," I said to myself. "I've got to forget him." So I started to drink. To help me forget. Fernet Branca. Yuk ... so bitter! But I forced it down like medicine. *(Poignant)* All alone in here with the bitter Fernet, my bitter regrets, the radio blaring away, the telephone ringing and my brother in law honking.

Honking from offstage

There he goes again! *(Goes to door and puts head in)* What is it? *(Loud honking)* No, be quiet! I told you I don't have time ... I'm talking to a friend of mine. *(Furious honking. She shouts over it)* Don't be so rude!

She slams the door. The honking continues behind it

Listen to him swearing at me with that horn. *(Shouts)* One of these days I'll throw him down the stairs, him *and* his wheelchair! *(Hysterical honking. She shouts louder)* All four floors! *(The honking subsides)* I should think so too. Now where was I? Oh yes, I was drunk on the Fernet Branca. Well not really drunk, just a bit sloshed. The doorbell rang. It was the boy's mother! I didn't know where to put

myself. Then she said, "Signora, forgive me but my son is dying of love for you. He can't eat, can't sleep, can't drink ... save his life! At least come and see him." *(Pause. Then dramatic)* What could I do? I'm a mother myself. *(Pause)* I went. Like a mother. I came into his room and there he was in bed ... so thin, so white! He burst into tears. I burst into tears. His mother burst into tears. Then she went out. *(Pause. Closes her eyes)* He hugs me and I hug him. He kisses me, I kiss him. And then. *(Opens her eyes, shouts)* "Stop!" He got another one of those shocks. "Listen," I said, "I like you too. I'm not ashamed to say it. As a matter of fact *(Getting louder and louder until she's bellowing)* I love you I love you I love you I LOVE YOU. *(To woman opposite)* The Fernet Branca. *(Then confidential)* Do you know they told me afterwards that everybody in that building rushed to their windows. "Who's in love?" "Somebody in love on the first floor?" "No, nobody here. It must be on the fourth. Who's in love up on four?" Wasn't I silly. Lucky nobody there knew me. *(Bellowing again)* "I love you but I can't make love with you. I've got two children, one husband and a brother in law!" Well he jumped out of bed. *(Pause)* Naked. *(Claps hands over her eyes but peeks)* Oh how naked he was! He grabbed a knife that happened to be there at the time and he held it against his throat. He said "If you won't make love to me, I'll kill myself!" *(Turns palms up in helpless gesture)* I'm not a murderess! *(Then tenderly)* So I got undressed and made love. Oh Signora, it was so beautiful, so delicate ... oh those kisses, those caresses ... God bless that knife!

Now as she talks she puts away ironing and ironing board

So that's how I discovered that love ... real love ... isn't that old business with me underneath and my husband on top bam bam bam ... the combine reaper! *(Langourous)* Love is sweet ... so sweet. *(Sighs)* I went back the next day. And the day after that and the day after that and all the days after the days after. What do you mean Signora? He was ill! I was simply stunned by the whole thing ... amazed. What? to get all the way to my age and find out the movies were true after all? *(Blissful)* I was going around in a total daze. *(Pause. Then irritable)* So my husband decided I must be drinking. And what does he do? Locks up the Fernet Branca. Brilliant, eh? But then he started to get really suspicious and he had me followed. One day I was in the boy's room standing there naked and he was standing there naked and we were just saying "Hello how are you?" "Fine and you?" And suddenly the door bursts open and in comes my husband. Fully dressed. I couldn't think what to

say so I said *(Polite and friendly)* "Fancy meeting you here." Well I was a bit rattled. I mean ...   , imagine! You standing there nude with a nude stranger and your husband in an overcoat. He started yelling that he was going to strangle the boy and yelling that he was going to strangle me. But my husband's only got two hands. So he grabbed both of us around the necks and squeezed our heads together. But even though I tried as hard as I could I couldn't die. I pushed my neck right up against the boy's. I closed my mouth tight so I wouldn't be able to breathe. *(Presses her lips together tightly to demonstrate)* Suddenly my nose started breathing off its own bat. I've got an independent nose! Then right in the middle of it all, in rushes the boy's mother and his sister and his granny and his aunt ... and me standing there starkers with my independent nose! I ran into the bathroom, locked the door, grabbed a razor blade and without a second thought I started cutting every vein I've got. I kept looking for more of them. Here's one ... zap! And another ... zap! One more ... one more ... zap zap zap! Who would have thought we had so many veins! I was even cutting them lengthwise so I'd die quicker. But my husband had this thing about how he wanted to kill me personally so he broke down the bathroom door. When he saw me covered in blood ... mine's very bright red ... I looked like

Dracula's Christmas dinner
... *then* he got frightened. So
he decided he'd save my life
instead of killing me and he
wrapped me up in a nice blanket ...
well he didn't want to get the car
messy ... and he took me to the
hospital. They sewed me up with
little cross stitches all over. I
looked like one of those old
fashioned samplers. On legs. And
my husband forgave me. He was
incredibly kind and incredibly
generous and incredibly under-
standing and then he locked me
up. What? Yes I know it's against
the law to lock your wife up but
what can I do? The police? You've
got a real bee in your bonnet about
calling the police don't you. Got a
relative in the force? Anyway I
couldn't do that because then the
whole story would get into the
papers. And then *(Counting on
fingers)* one, my husband would
divorce me, two he'd take my kids
away and three he'd leave me his
brother in exchange! No no, there's
nothing I can do. I just have to ...
oh excuse me.

*The telephone is ringing again. She
answers it crossly.*

Hello. *(Astonished)* Oh! *(Great
tenderness)* Darling why are you
phoning me? *(Shouts to woman
opposite)* It's the boy! *(Resumes
intimate tone)* You know you
mustn't call me, love, you know
that. How can I? How can I
possibly come and meet you when
I'm locked in? Oh it's all so ...

(Shouts) What? You can't! Are you
crazy? Now listen to me ... don't
you dare do such a ... hello? Hello!
He's hung up!
Rushes down to the window.

He's gone mad, Signora! He says he's
coming round here to pick the lock
with a bent nail. Well of course I
know it won't work but what about
the neighbours? How am I going to
look if somebody goes past in the
hall and sees him scratching away
at my keyhole with a bent nail?

Knocking at the front door

Oh my God it's him! He's here
already! *(Rushes to door. Shouts)*
Go away! My husband will be here
any minute. Go away! What? Who
is that? Money? What money? Oh!
(To woman opposite) Would you
believe it! It's the man my husband
phoned me about. The creditor! Oh
what a mess! *(Through door)*
There's nobody at home, no one's
here. Well yes I'm here but I'm
only the maid. What? Yes I did say
my husband was coming. Uh ...
he's the cook. No the family isn't
here. They've all gone! Where? Uh
... on a cruise. In the car. Listen
my orders are don't open the door
and don't speak to anybody and
don't turn on the radio and don't
watch T.V. And anyway even if I
did want to open the door I
couldn't because I haven't got the
key. *(To woman opposite
anxiously)* Oh Lord, now what have
I said! *(Through door)* What? Well
yes they do lock me in, yes. Uh ...
because ... because my mistress

thinks I steal from them. No no
don't worry about that! I'm not
starving to death ... they leave me
emergency rations. The police?
Why do you want to call the
police? *(To herself)* He must be
related to the lady opposite.
(Through door) Hey listen, come
back! Come back! *(Pause)* Gone.

*She comes downstage to the
window*

He said he was going to get the
police. I bet he was only bluffing.
Trying to scare me. How does he
think I'm going to know what my
husband's been up to? He never
tells me anything.

Knocking at the front door

Oh here we go again. Who's it going
to be this time? The creditor? The
police? That crazy boy? Well I'm
not going to answer it. I'm not
going to open the door for any of
them!

The knocking gets more insistent

Maybe it really is the police.

*A man's voice shouts 'Maria!
Maria!'*

My husband! That's my husband's
voice. *(Goes to door)* Aldo, why
are you knocking? I know the
bell's broken again but you've got
your key so open the door. What?
You've lost your keys? *(Dramatic)*
Oh my God what'll happen to me
now? I *will* starve to death ...
buried alive in here with only the
baby and your brother in law's
hand. What a terrible terrible

death! *(Then furious)* Anyway
you'd better look out! Your friend
was here just now. That one you
owe the money to ... that's right.
He's gone to call the police. No no
no I didn't say a word to him not a
single word ... I'm not an idiot. He
only talked to the maid. What do
you mean we haven't got a maid.
We've got a maid all right! Me!
Maid, nurse, babysitter, cook,
charlady, washerwoman and
screwing machine! No I am not
hysterical and I'm not crazy either.
(Hysterically) I'll be glad when the
police do come. That'll put an end
to the whole thing. Yes do ... do
go away! Go! Go! Go away and
stay away you ... you ... you ...
*(Makes frustrated muttering and
growling sounds searching for the
right epithet)* ... you astigmatic!
(Then stamps her foot) Oh!

*She comes back downstage,
depressed.*

Honestly, all the swear words I know
and when I really need a good one
that's all I can come out with.
Astigmatic! And he's got perfect
vision. Oh I feel such a fool.
(Shrugs) Well anyway, I said what
I thought for once. *(Baby cries
offstage)* The baby! *(Very alarmed)*
Signora, listen ... the baby's
crying! What? *(Heading for
bedroom)* You bet I'm scared. He's
never cried since he was born!

*Opens bedroom door and goes in.
Sound of baby crying and high
mass on T.V. She turns off T.V.
sound of a honk or two*

(Shouts) You! What are you doing in my room? Oh how could you? Coming in and waking my baby just to get me in here. Stop! Stop that! Leave me alone! (To baby) Don't cry, precious. (Shouts again) I said leave me alone, you!

The telephone rings. She dashes out, her negligee torn

That slob! Look what he's done to my new negligee! (To phone) All right I'm coming I'm coming. (Over her shoulder back toward bedroom) Just you wait till your brother comes home! (to herself) If he comes home.

Picks up phone

Hello. Oh no! (Fury) Listen if you don't stop ringing me up I swear to God I'll put a bomb in the telephone. I'll blow your gums off! Oh you filthy disgusting horrible pig aren't you ashamed of yourself? I'm a mother! How would you feel if somebody said all those terrible things to your lovely white haired old mother knitting in front of the fire. (Pause) Ha! That stopped him. Found the right word at last. The magic word that beats in the heart of every decent Italian man ... Mama! (Operatic) Mama! (Pause) What? (Puts down the phone) He's an orphan. (Then to woman opposite indignantly) And what about my brother in law? Look what he's done to my ... oh. (Breaks off) Signora! Hey Signora! (Dejected) She's gone. (Her gaze goes up and she sees the peeping

tom) But look who's back.

The baby cries offstage. As she goes up to the bedroom door she picks up the rifle.

Don't cry. Mama's going to show you how to kill a peeping tom.

Knocking at the door

(To peeping tom) Don't go ... I'll be right back. (Goes to door) Who's there? Oh my God, for pity's sake go away. I'm expecting my husband. And the police. And some crazy creditor. Go away! Don't touch that lock with your nail do you hear me? Oh well it doesn't matter you'll never get it open with ... (Shouts) you've opened it! (As the door starts to open she quickly puts the chain across) You can't get in. I've put the chain up. Oh help!

She turns and looks gladly over to the window

Oh Signora ... you've come back! Listen this crazy boy's got the door open with that nail. I've got the chain up but what do you think I should— (Breaks off as boy's hand appears through the crack of the door, outraged) Leave my house this minute with that hand!

The hand beckons insistently

Now what? You want to shake hands? Listen I keep telling you my husband's coming! Oh you're so stubborn. Here. You can hold my hand but only for a minute. I have to ... (Breaks off) ouch! What are you doing?

The boy is pulling her toward him.

Stop pulling me. Let me go! *(The baby cries again offstage)* The baby's crying. It's time for his cereal. Let go! *(Pulls herself free)* Now go away. Just go away and lock the door again with that bent nail of yours. No, wait. Leave the nail downstairs with the caretaker ... my husband's lost his keys.

The baby cries. She goes to the bedroom door.

All right, sweetie, Mama's going to get your cereal right this minute.

Goes toward kitchen. Sees the boy's hand still sticking through door.

What? Haven't you gone yet? Right. You asked for it. *(Goes into kitchen and comes out with huge plastic spoon)* Look out! I'm going to slice all your fingers off!

She bangs the spoon down on his hand. He yells. She stares at his hand, then at the spoon. To woman opposite.

Hey Signora ... I stabbed him with a spoon! *(Looks at spoon again, amazed)* What should I do? What did you say? Take a patent out on it? Oh ... put disinfectant on it. *(Takes boy's hand)* Yes of course, I'll get some. Oh certainly, I've got plenty. My husband gives me everything I need.

Gets disinfectant and cotton wool and puts it on boy's hand

Keep still, it won't hurt you. It's the kind you use for babies. Oh darling ... what an awful cut I gave you. Now you must go away, you must. Oh all right, one little kiss. *(Kisses his hand)* On your mouth? Certainly not. You're not getting anything on your mouth. And no I am not taking this chain off. Oh help help!

He has pulled her so hard toward him that her face is mashed up against the crack in the door.

Stop! My head won't go through there! I've got ears remember! Wait wait wait ... oh I never knew anybody so stubborn ... wait! I'll try and get my head through sideways.

She manages to get her head part way through the crack

Oh my God I'm stuck! My head's stuck in the door! Don't pull ... push! *(Then muffled)* Not with your mouth, fool, with your hand! Ouch! Ouch! Ouch!

Her head comes back through the door with the last 'ouch'. She holds her face in her hands

My poor face ... it's all scratched. *(As she moves away from the door the boy beats frantically on the door with his outside hand)* Will you please stop! This is no time for your drum practice. Just go! Go away! *(The arm in the crack of the door waves wildly about)* What? You're stuck now? I don't believe this! *(To woman opposite)* Signora, guess what! His arm's stuck in the door. It's a disaster. *(Melodramatic)* He'll grow old with his arm stuck in my house. My husband will kill me! What am I going to do? What? Soapy water? Oh yes, yes of course ... like for rings.

Goes toward kitchen. Looks up and once more sees peeping tom

He's still up there. *(Shouts)* Go away! *(To woman opposite)* Hot soapy water do you think? Yes hot'll work better. *(Then furious to peeping tom)* Lesbian! *(Then to herself)* Calm down. Just calm down. Now. *(Deep breath)* Who wants what? *(Then rapidly pointing first at peeping tom)* He wants a sexy peep. *(Then at boy's arm)* He wants hot water. *(Then at the baby who cries offstage)* He wants his cereal. *(Then toward brother in law offstage who honks)* And he wants a grope. Does that take care of all the men around here? *(Telephone rings)* Oh yes ... and *he* wants a pornographic chat. *(Picks up phone. Speaks with great sweetness)* Hello you depraved, disgusting, degenerate pig ... whoops. *(Then with nervous cheer)* Hello dear. What? *(Pause)* Who is that? Oh sorry, I thought it was my husband ... no I mean I didn't think it was my husband ... what I mean is ... *(Deep breath. Then courteously efficient)* I'm afraid my husband's not at home just at the moment. May I take a message? Oh yes. Yes I see. Mmmm hmmm. *(Then*

laughs heartily) Terrific! Congratulations and let's hope it's a boy but you've got the wrong number. What? Yes a man does live here as a matter of fact. My husband. But my husband only gets *me* pregnant. You're what? You're positive? Your daughter? No he did not happen to mention it to me. My God he's the depraved, disgusting degenerate ... *(Breaks off)* How old is your daughter anyway? Sixteen. Oh ... right. Not quite sixteen. Great. Marvellous. Look, maybe instead of letting your not quite sixteen year old daughter run around getting pregnant by other peoples' husbands you should try locking her up! I'm over sixteen myself and my husband locks me up so why don't you think about ... what? How dare you! *(Bangs down the phone. To woman opposite)* He called me a whore! His daughter gets pregnant by my husband and he calls me a whore!

The boy bangs loudly on the door from the outside again

Leave me alone, I've got family problems. My husband's pregnant.

Goes into kitchen. Baby cries. Brother in law honks. She comes out of the kitchen with a basin of water in one hand and a bowl of cereal in the other.

All right I'm coming I'm coming! Ooooh ... ouch! This cereal's hot. *(Goes into bedroom)* Hello sweetheart, here's Mama with your nice cereal. Stop! Stop that! take that hand off me this minute! Look out, you'll spill the cereal. Look out! *(A scream)* Oh my God!

She rushes on with the basin of water which she puts down. Then to woman opposite.

I've spilled hot cereal right on his eyes! No not the baby, my brother in law. What shall I do? Nivea cream? Oh yes, good idea. Oh sure I've got lots of it. *(Getting the cream)* I told you my husband gives me everything I need.

The boy bangs on the door again.

Leave me alone, I said. I'm busy. I've been burning my brother in law.

She goes into the bedroom and comes out again wheeling her brother in law, a dummy covered in plaster of paris except for one large hand and sitting in a wheelchair with an auto horn attached to one arm of it. She puts ointment on the dummy's eyes.

Well I'm sorry it hurts but it was your own fault really. I told you it was going to spill but you just went on and ... stop that! Unhand me!

She has manipulated the dummy's arm so that it clutches her

Let me go this minute ... let me go! *(Reaches for the basin of water)* I'm warning you! *(Holds basin threateningly over the dummy's head)* There's boiling water in this basin! *(The hand lets her go)* So!

Finally got the message, eh? Good.

Runs over to the boy with the basin.

Quick put your arm in here. No of course it's not boiling. I just said that to frighten my brother in law.

The boy puts his arm in, screams and pulls it out of the water and out of the crack in the door. She looks at the basin, surprised

Oh. So it was boiling. Never mind you got your arm out. Well I'm sorry it hurts but it'll only be a little scald. Put some of this on. Here. *(Hands Nivea cream through the door)* And then go away. Please. I mean it. *(Then shouts)* What are you doing?

She is being pulled up against the door by the boy

Let me go! Stop! Have you gone mad? What are you doing? Let me go. If anybody sees us we'll all three get sent to prison. You, me and the door! Let go ... you haven't got any respect for me at all. I'm going to make you very sorry for this. I'll punish you. Oh you don't believe me? Well get this!

She pulls the boy towards her with all her strength and slams the door on him. There is a yell of pain and his footsteps running away. She stands still for a moment, then takes the chain off the door and opens it wide. Looks out. Shuts door sadly and comes back to the window.

They're all the same. Love ... ha! He's just like all the others. Only after one thing. *(Despair)* I can't bear it! I just can't bear it! *(Baby cries again offstage)* My baby ... he's the only one I really love. I'll go to my baby.

As she starts for the bedroom the phone rings

Shut up! Just shut up!

Brother in law honks

And you shut up too! Shut up! Shut up!

The crying, the honking and the phone ringing all get louder and louder. She covers her ears and screams

Stop! Stop! Stop! I've had enough!

And she runs and gets the rifle and points it at her throat.

I've had enough!

Total silence. She stands still, her eyes closed. Then she opens her eyes and turns to look at the woman opposite

(Dazed) What? *(Lowers the gun)* Yes ... yes. *(Holding back tears)* Oh my God, my God what was I thinking of! *(Puts gun down)* Thank heaven you came to live opposite. *(More cheerful as she listens)* Yes? Yes? Oh yes what marvellous advice! I'll do it. I'll do it right now.

Brother in law honks and she goes over to him, smiling

I'm coming honey. *(Strokes him*

suggestively) I'm right here. Ready and willing! Tell you what ... let's go for a walk to the park and have some fun just the two of us, eh? *(Pushing wheelchair to door)* To the bushes!

She opens the door and gives the wheelchair a hard shove. We hear it bumping down the stairs and the horn honking as it goes

One! Two! Three! Oh ... watch out! Watch out for the picture window on the mezzanine floor!

There is a terrific crash of glass. Then silence. To woman opposite.

Well ... that's one down.

The baby cries offstage and she starts to go to him again. Then stops and looks up at peeping tom. Waves and blows him kisses. Moves voluptuously toward the window, smiling and wiggling her hips. Then grabs the rifle fast and shoots.

(Shouts) That's one in the eye for you, Peeper!

Baby cries again and once more she goes toward the bedroom. The phone rings. Furious, she picks it up and speaks in a terrible voice.

Hello!

Pause. Then very sweetly.

Oh Aldo, hello. Yes everything's just fine. Yes yes I'm quite calm. No there's nobody here, Aldo, nothing but peace and quiet. Come on up. I'm expecting you.

*Hangs up. Then to woman
opposite.*

Don't worry, Signora, I am calm.
Absolutely calm.

*She gets the rifle and takes up a
position leaning against the table
with the rifle pointing at the front
door. Very carefully she takes aim.*

I'm just waiting here very very
calmly.

End of play

The Same Old Story

Music. (Je t'aime, moi non plus possibly.) Lights up on a woman who is lying on her back on a rostrum downstage writhing and struggling.

No no please! Please stop! Not like that, I can't breathe! You're squashing me. Will you stop slobbering into my neck like that? No and not in my ear! Yes I did say I liked it ... I do ... but not with your tongue whizzing around in there like an egg beater. And you can just stop that too. My God how many hands have you got? Let me breathe ... I can't breathe! Get off me!

She sits up as though extricating herself out from under a man.

Phew! At last! Ding ding! *(Then referee voice)* Into your corners! *(Then as to the man)* Is that what you call making love? Yes as a matter of fact I do enjoy making love only shouldn't there be a little love in it? Oh right. Of course. I'm being romantic and sentimental. You would say that. Well get this ... I am not a pinball machine. You can't just put your money in the slot and start bashing away and expect all my lights to light up. You start getting rough with me and I go into Tilt, see?

Annoyed, she stands up.

It's incredible. If a girl doesn't get straight down on her back, skirt up, pants down, legs open and raring to go she's an uptight bitch with a *(then very rapidly)* repressed moralistic attitude to sex inculcated by a reactionary imperialist ecclesiastical royalist conformist education. Oh? You think I'm being clever? You mean I'm being intelligent and intelligent women are ball breakers right? You'd rather have a dumb blonde who giggles. And wiggles.

She rotates her hips and laughs suggestively. Then mimes angrily pushing his hands away as he starts to touch her up.

Don't touch me, I said. You really get on my nerves. Leave me alone! Leave me alone!

A pause. Then, arms outstretched and rotating her hips again she sings softly and very suggestively:

Allons enfant de la Patrie ... *(Then, eyes closed and making a pretence of pushing his hands away again)* I said take your hands off me. Didn't you hear me say I didn't want you, you idiot? *(And now gradually sinking to a sitting and then a lying position)* Don't touch me like that. Don't. Don't. Don't ... *(Then languid and increasingly voluptuous)* No no no I'm not really mad at you. Yes let's do it. Let's make love. When you want to you can be so sweet. Almost human. A real comrade ... mmmmm. I feel good with you. We talk about things that matter. With you I get to use my brain ... I'm really fulfilled with you. You don't just care about me because of the way I make love. You like the way I think and the way I talk. *(More and more erotically)* After we make love you like us to talk so we talk. It's nice. I talk and you listen and you talk and I ... and I ... and I ... and I ... *(She is clearly reaching her climax but now she breaks off suddenly and says flatly)* get pregnant.

Then as though pushing the man off herself.

Stop! Wait! I have to tell you something. No no ... it's important! I'm not on the pill. Well I came off it. It was making my tits as big as the dome of St Peter's. *(Then reluctant)* Well okay let's go on then but be careful.

Don't forget what happened that other time ... oh God it was so terrible! Yes all right I know you felt terrible too but I felt worse! Much much worse, okay? So be careful. *(She lies quite still in silence but then starts drumming her fingers nervously. Staccato)* Be careful! *(Silence again. Then shouts it)* Be careful! Well I'm sorry but I can't relax. I've got a block about it now thinking about pregnancy. Diaphragm? Yes I have a diaphragm but I do need advance warning, you know. Anyway it really turns me off having that rubber thing inside me ... like chewing gum.

Then as if watching the man get up.

Oh you've lost your inspiration. Sorry. *(Then thoughtful)* But it's funny when you think about it. I don't want to get pregnant and he loses his inspiration!

She sits up beginning to get angry.

And you're supposed to be the big militant radical. Do me a favour. Do you know what you are? A big radical prick. Yes and that's who your real comrade is ... your prick! That's the one who's a reactionary imperialist ecclesiastical capitalist royalist ... puppet! *(Pointing)* Take a good look at it, go on! See? It's got a cardinal's cap on! And stripes like a general. And it's making the fascist salute. *(She raises a clenched fist)* Yes I did say fascist! What? *(She starts to cry)* Don't be so mean, you bastard. No! No I do not think with my uterus. Yes I'm crying. You've hurt my feelings.

She lies down suddenly as though she's been pushed down.

Oh terrific. It turns you on when I cry. *(Then getting excited herself)* Yes Yes I know you love me ... yes I love you too ... yes let's go on let's go on. *(then languid and voluptuous again)* I know it isn't your fault. It's society's fault, oh I know that. The exploitation, the materialism, the consumerism, the multinational corporations, the ... *(Breaks off, anxious)* Stop, please stop. *(Then shouts)* Stop stop stop! *(Pause. Then tonelessly)* You didn't stop. Now I'm pregnant. *(Pushing him away)* I am pregnant, I know it. *(Shouts wildly)* I'm pregnant!

She sits up and folds her hands in her lap. Now in a doctor's office.

Yes Doctor I'm pregnant. Three months. Yes I've had the test. Yes I'll lie down but please be gentle with me. Yes I know this kind of examination doesn't hurt but I'm very tense. I've already had one abortion. They didn't give me any anaesthetic ... not even a local. I was wide awake the whole time. The pain was horrible! But the worst thing was the way they treated me. Like a whore. Wouldn't even let me scream. "Shut up! It's all your own fault. Now you have to pay for it." *(Then wryly, rubbing her fingers together)* And did I pay!

Sits up.

This time I want my abortion done right. I don't want to feel anything. I want a general anaesthetic and I don't even want to know when you do it. Just knock me out a week beforehand and whenever it's convenient and you've got a minute or two to spare you can ... *(Breaks off, appalled)* A million lire! The price of everything is going up, eh? Yes yes I know, Doctor. The nursing home, the anaesthetic, yes and the risk you're taking yes yes ... but a million lire! Try the new abortion law? Oh come on! Anyway I've tried it. I nearly went mad trying to find any doctor who'd write me an abortion certificate ... not to speak of a hospital where they'd put me on their waiting list. And when my name finally did come up it turned out that everybody in that hospital was *(Sarcastic)* A Defender of The Unborn Life! Bunch of conscientious objectors. The nurses objected, the cleaners objected and the cook! He objected the most! We would've all starved to death if it hadn't been for some girls that turned up to do a pro-abortion sit-in at the hospital. Then the police came along and threw the girls out. I got scared, I'll tell you. I thought, "If I wait for this new law to help me I'll end up giving birth to a twenty four year old son who's finished his military service is unemployed and all set to emi-grate to West Germany!' ... So I got out ... quick. *(Pause)* A million lire ... Well now I can see why all the doctors have got onto this defend life number. At a million lire per defence they can all become millionaires. On us!

She stands up suddenly.

No. I'm not going through with it. Oh I could get somebody to lend me the money. That's not it. But this is blackmail! There's a law now and it ought to be respected! I'll keep it, Doctor. Every woman ought to have a baby isn't that right. I'll keep it. Then I'll be fulfilled won't I. Fulfilled! Fulfilled! *(Shouting it)* Fulfilled!

Jumps up onto the rostrum with her back to the audience. Marches in place and shouts.

Motherhood! Motherhood! Third month! Fourth month! Fifth month!

Then turns to face the audience.

The belly's swelling up, the tits are getting bigger. *(Then in an official sounding voice)* Pre-Natal Exercises For The Successful Pregnancy. *(Demonstrating)* Knee bends! One two three four! And again! One two three four! Now down on your back. Get those legs up in the air! One two three four! Pant like a dog. *(Pants)* Faster! *(She pants faster and faster and then flops back, exhausted)* Oh God I feel awful, I think I'm going to be sick. I'm dizzy ... I feel terrible.

Holds her stomach with her hands. Then her face lights up.

It moved! The little bugger moved! It's fluttering inside me. Oh that's beautiful. So beautiful!

She sits up. Passionate.

Ice cream! Ice cream! I want ice cream with a cherry on top and sphaghetti and whipped cream and water melon and salami!

Then in the brisk professional tone again.

A strong sound straight from the abdomen now please. Aaaaah! Louder. Aaaaah! Louder. Aaaaah. *(And she bends over holding her stomach)* It's starting. Oh, it hurts!

Slowly she lies down on the rostrum her head toward the audience.

Yes Sister, I'm lying down. Yes I'm relaxed, Sister. Yes I'll do my shallow breathing, Sister. *(Pants)* Yes yes yes I'll push! Oh! Oh! Oh! It hurts, I can't stand it! It hurts! *(She stops screaming and looks round the stage)* Where's he? Him! Where's the father? What? Outside? What's he doing outside? *(Pause)* Oh yes?

She sits up. Speaks with friendly cynicism to the audience.

Smoking nervously. *(Exaggerated compassion)* Oh the poor thing! He's all tense and nervous. *(Pause)* Wish he'd been less tense and more nervous nine months ago!

Then in relaxed conversational tones.

I don't know about you but it really gets me down the way it's always the woman that gets pregnant. Never the man. *I* object! Actually it's a real obsession with me. I even dream about it. The other night I dreamed that my boyfriend had breasts. Fantastic big round breasts. I couldn't wait to get my hands on them but he said *(Little petulant voice)* "Leave me alone or I'll tell my mother!" And then he told me that he was something called a "She-Man". This was a special kind of man who gets pregnant if he has sex with a woman and hasn't taken precautions.

Turns as to the boyfriend, mimes stroking his breasts and gently forcing him to lie down. Speaks with erotic urgency.

Oh you're lovely. So soft and lovely! Go on take your clothes off and lie down ... I want to talk to you. *(Lies as though on top of him)* Why are you so nervous love, hmmm? You're not on the pill? Never mind it doesn't matter. Doesn't matter at all, I love you just the same. Oh you're so beautiful! You're afraid of getting pregnant? Oh listen don't worry, baby, don't worry. I'll take care of you. Oh this is terrific I never want to stop. You can probably get a legal abortion, just don't worry! Come on ... come on! And if you

can't I'll pay for one. Oh sure total anaesthetic ... everything! You won't feel a thing. Mmmmmmm! Or if you want to keep the baby I'll marry you. Come on let's do it ... let's do it. Let's make love! It doesn't matter about getting pregnant. After all, a man's really only truly fulfilled when he becomes a mother. *(Then shouts it)* A mother! Mother! Mother!

She sits up.

It's born! *(Glad relief)* It's born! Is it a boy? *(Pause)* No? *(Then as if flabbergasted)* What is it? *(Pause. Then philosophic)* Oh well I can still love her.

Now she sits facing the audience and holding the imaginary baby and miming the following as the midwife.

Smack baby's bottom. Smack smack! Make it cry. Wah wah! Cut the cord. Snip snip! Now tie the knot. Round and round! Dip into hot water. Splash splash! Now into cold water. Brr brr! Don't cry now, don't cry. Onto the scales with you. Almost four kilos! What a fine baby!

She hands the baby over as to the mother and then as the mother takes it.

Come to Mama! Who's a lovely baby girl? Who's my baby then? Time for your feed, time for your vaccination, time for your injection, now time for an enema, oh what a beautiful poo! Clever

girl! Oops she's being sick. Time
for another feed, time to bring the
wind up, time to take your
vitamins, time to go to sleep, time
to wake up. Smile for Mama!
Smile! Don't cry! Look at your
lovely toys. Oh what lovely toys for
baby. Wuzza wuzza wuzza. No no
mustn't throw them around. Play
with the toys ... that's the way,
there's a honey bunny! Time for
your cereal. Oh naughty! Don't
spit it out. Lovely cereal. Yummy
yummy! Oh mustn't throw the
spoon on the floor. No no no! Eat
your lovely cereal and grow up and
be Mama's big girl. Grow up!
Grow up!

*She mimes sitting the baby beside
her.*

STOP.

Now sit still and I'll tell you a lovely
story. Listen. Once upon a time
there was a pretty little girl who
had a beautiful dolly. Well actually
the dolly wasn't beautiful at all she
was hideous. Dirty and nearly bald
and made out of old rags but the
little girl loved her. She used to
talk to the dolly all the time and
the dolly would talk back to her.
Yes! The dolly could talk! But the
only thing she talked was terrible
swearing and awful rude words.
And the little girl learned all the
words and she said them too. Her
mother was horrified. "Who taught
you that disgusting language?"
"My dolly taught me." "Oh what
a fib! You've been running around
with bad little boys haven't you.
Dollies don't use naughty words."

"Mine does," said the little girl.
"Here, Dolly, say some dirty word
for my mother." Now the dolly
always did everything the little girl
told her to do because she loved
her, so she brought out a whole
stream of terrible swear words.
"Bitch! Bastard! Shithead!
Fuckface! Asshole asshole
asshole!" Oh! The little girl's
mother went red in the face and
she grabbed the dolly and threw
her out of the window into a
garbage dump that was in the field
outside. "Bad mama bad mama!"
shouted the little girl and she ran
down the stairs and out into the
field. Too late! Before she could
pick up the dolly a big mean
looking cat grabbed it. A ginger
cat. A red! And he ran off into the
woods with the dolly in his mouth.
Crying and crying the little girl
went after him. She walked and she
walked and she walked and she
searched and she searched and she
searched. It got dark and she got
lost in the woods which had turned
into a huge scarey forest. Then far
far away in the distance she saw a
tiny little light. So she walked
toward the light and when she got
near to it what did she see? A
dwarf! A little bitty dwarf standing
on top of a big toadstool and
peeing a stream of phosphorescent
pee! "Oh dwarf, little dwarf, have
you seen a big red cat carrying a
dolly who uses terrible language."
"There he is," says the dwarf, still
peeing and he sends his
phosphorescent pee right onto the

ginger cat and ... zammo! ... the cat falls down dead! Well, as everybody knows, dwarf's pee is terrifically poisonous for cats. "Oh thank you, thank you" says the little girl and she hugs her dolly who's all soaked in pee. But the dolly starts shouting. "Who's this fucking shitface dwarf? Who does this bastard asshole think he is, killing my bad red cat. I loved that cat! He beat the hell out of me and he ripped me off. He never stopped bossing me around and he made me work till I dropped. He did horrible things to me but I loved him all the same. He treated me like dirt, like a slave! Oh how I suffered. I cried all the time but I loved him even more. He made me feel like a real woman with a man like other women have. And now what am I going to do without my bad red cat? Oh you stupid prick of a dwarf, you shithead bastard, what am I going to fucking well do now?" "Oh I'm crazy about this dirty mouth dolly," shouts the dwarf. "I just love her. I think I'll marry her." "No," said a terrible deep voice out of the dark scarey shadows of the forest no longer lit up by the dwarf's phosphorescent pee, "I'm going to marry her." Who could it be? Oh how terrible, it's a great big huge wolf with great big huge teeth. *(Makes a growling bark)* "I'll marry her." "I don't want him" says the dolly. "I'm not going to marry that silly cocksucker." "I'm not a silly cocksucker," says the wolf, "I'm

an electronic engineer. A wicked witch turned me into a wolf. As a matter of fact I've still got my lampograph pen that I take with me everywhere. Now if this little virgin girl would be so kind as to kiss me on the forehead I will immediately turn into a good looking young professional man grammar school educated and with impeccable references seeking warmth and companionship." So the little girl kissed the wolf and ... zammo! ... out jumps an unbelievably handsome electronic engineer who was so happy he let off an enormous fart right in the dwarf's face and the dwarf fell down dead. Well as everybody knows, electronic engineer's farts are terrifically poisonous for dwarves. Now the minute she clapped eyes on the engineer the little girl fell in love with him. "Oh what a handsome engineer!" she cried. Well time had gone by and the little girl was grown up and had those round things that women have in the front and she was round behind as well and it's well known that engineers are wild about these round things. It's a real professional vocation with them. So the good looking young engineer with the lampograph pen in his inside pocket said "I've changed my mind. I won't marry the doll. I'll marry the little girl with the bouncy tits and the nice round ass." "What about this fucking wanker then?" says the dolly. "He's jilted me already." So the engineer and the little girl-woman got married and lived happily ever after. And the next day the dolly said "I'm calling a union meeting. Union meeting everybody! Now listen my dear shithead bride and groom, this happy-ever-after crap has got to stop. I'm sick of all this smooching and slobbering and fucketty-fuck. I just get left out because you're always at it. He goes off every day to do his electronic engineering and you just hang around with your little round ass yearning for him to come home again. And when he does get home he throws you on the bed and it's fucketty fuck fuck fuck. Then it's fucketty fuck in the mornings before you get up and it's fucketty fuck again after lunch which just so happens to be very bad for your health." "But I'm so happy," says the little girl-bride whose tummy had already got all big and round. "I'm so in love." "Balls!" says the dolly. "Don't give me that horse shit 'I'm happy I'm happy'. I've never seen such a dumb miserable twat in my life. You're even a dumber twat than me when I was living with my bad red cat but at least with him you could fight things out on a political level. But with this asshole of an engineer what's there to fight? He doesn't beat you up but he leaves you here alone all day like some stupid fucking puppet *and* he never even talks to you which is even worse you silly shithead." "Listen you lousy rag doll," yells the good

looking young professional man grammar school educated with impeccable references searching for warmth and companionship. "You just shut your dirty mouth or I'll flush you down the bog." "Terrific" says the dolly. "You should go to the bog as a matter of fact and get rid of some of that shit you're so full of." "Right I will," says the engineer, "But you're coming with me. I'll use you for toilet paper." And he takes the dolly off to the bathroom and locks the door. "No please don't, my darling hubby. Don't do a thing like that to my dolly. Open the door." "No I won't. I'm sitting here with my pants down and now I'm going to wipe my ass with this rag doll." The very next moment there's a terrible scream. Aaaaaah! An electronic scream! The engineer! What do you think had happened? As soon as he started to wipe his bottom with the dolly ... zammo! ... she shot up his bumhole! Up up up until only her feet were sticking out. "Help me, help me, wife! This wicked spiteful dolly has shoved herself up my bottom. Pull her out. Pull!" "I am pulling but I can't get her out." "Aaaaaah!" screams the engineer. "It hurts! I feel like I'm dying! No! I feel like I'm giving birth! Call the midwife!" Out goes the little girl-woman to find a midwife. But when she opens the door ... well the ways of the Lord are infinite as is well known ... who should happen to be passing but a midwife! "Oh heaven has sent you. Please come in. We've got a family problem." Well when the midwife came face to face with the engineer's backside she says "Is this your husband?" "Yes it is." "Well it's going to be a tricky delivery," she says. "Breech presentation. Feet first." And she falls about laughing. *(To audience)* Now you know what happens to us women when we get a fit of the giggles. "Help! I have to pee! I have to pee!" shouts the midwife. "Listen," she says. "I've been put under a terrible spell and when I start peeing I can't stop. Help me! I don't want to cause floods and disasters. Help help! I don't want to be responsible for any casualties. Fetch me a bucket." So they get her a bucket and she does all her pee in it in a very dignified way. "Now give this to your husband to drink," she says. "It's magic. It'll move his bowels." "Is everybody insane in this house I should drink the pee of a midwife that I don't even know?" says the engineer. "But you must move your bowels," she says to him. "Well okay then but put some vermouth in it and some marsala and angostura bitters and a couple of beaten up eggs ... hey it's good! Would you believe it ... it's good!" And he drank and he drank and he drank and his belly got bigger and bigger and bigger until ... zammo! ... he exploded. Just completely

blew up. Not a single scrap of him left. Not even his lampograph pen that had always been so faithful to him. But there was the dolly all in one piece laughing like mad. "There you are you fucking idiot, you're free!" she says to the little girl. "Now you've got your own body and your own choices and you belong to yourself again. You're free! Come on let's get out of here. Let's go!" The grown up little girl picked up the dolly and she hugged her and hugged her until the dolly disappeared right into her heart. And now the grown up little girl was alone, walking down a long long road. She walked and she walked and she walked until she came to a big tree and under the tree there were a lot of little grown up girls just like her. They gave her a big welcome. "Sit down," they said. "Stay with us. We're all going to tell each other our life stories. You begin," they said to a little blond girl who was sitting there with them. So she began. "When I was a little girl I had a rag dolly who was always swearing and saying dirty words ..." "Ha ha ha!" And all the little girls sitting in the circle burst out laughing. "How funny, oh how funny! Who'd believe it? We've all got the same story to tell. It's the same old story for us all!"

End of play

Medea

Help! Help! Come quickly you
women ... hurry! Medea's locked
herself up in her house with her
two little children and she's
screaming and ranting like a
madwoman. She's demented! She
won't listen to reason. You'd think
she'd been bitten by a tarantula,
her eyes are so wild ... they're
starting right out of her head. She's
frantic with jealousy because her
man, Jason, is leaving her for a
younger woman. He's going to
marry her and Medea can't accept
it. She just won't believe that now
she has to leave her home and give
up her children. She has to! But
she won't be reasonable. Medea!
Medea, come to the door, I want
to talk to you. Listen woman, be
sensible! Stop thinking about
yourself and think of your
children. Don't you see? With this
new marriage they'll be much
better off. A nicer place to live,
lovely clothes and always enough to
eat on the table. They'll have a
grand new name and they'll be
respected by all the best people.
This new family is going to live in
the King's palace! Oh listen Medea,
if you love your children you'll
sacrifice yourself for them. Think
like a good mother—not like a
proud woman. For the sake of
your own flesh and blood, resign
yourself. After all, you haven't
been humiliated ... you aren't
despised. Your husband talks about
you with the greatest respect
wherever he goes. He says you're
the best of women. He says no one
could have been more kind and
loving to his children or to him. He
says he'll always care about you.
Well, Medea? Say something.
Can't you answer? Open the door.
Come out and talk to us. Don't
you know that we've suffered the
same fate as you and wept the
same tears? Our men have betrayed
us too. We understand you,
Medea! Stand back. She's decided
to come to the door. Here she is.
Oh my God, her face is so pale ...
and her hands! White! As if all the
blood's been drained out of her.
Catch her—she'll fall! Here ... sit
on the step, Medea. Stand back!
Give her room you women, let her
breathe! Quiet! Hush! She wants to
say something. Speak to us Medea,

we're listening. Ah ... she can't make a sound after all that screaming. Give her some water ... her throat's dry. There. That's better. Now talk to us, Medea, it will do you good. Don't hold back. Speak.

h women ... my friends ... tell me what she's like, my husband's new woman. I only saw her once, in the distance and she looked so beautiful ... so young. I was young like that, young and fresh—you know I was! I was only sixteen when Jason first knew me. I had long black hair and my skin was white and tender. My breasts were so round they burst out of my blouse, my neck was smooth, my cheeks full and my belly so flat and firm it didn't touch my skirt. My thighs were silky and my whole body was so soft and delicate that when he held me in his arms he was frightened that he'd bruise me or break me. His hand trembled when he touched me ... he trembled all over with fear that it would be sacrilege to make love to me.

'e've all known that time, Medea but that time is past! It's gone, it's over. And for us women our fate is certain. Our men will always go searching for new flesh, new breasts and a fresh young mouth. It's just the law of life.

he law? What is this law that you're sentencing me under? You tell me, you women. Did you invent it yourselves, my friends? Did you write down the words and have them proclaimed to the world? Did you beat the drum in the market place to announce that it was a sacred law? Men! Men! It's the men who created this law to use against us women. They signed it, they sealed it and they made it holy and binding under the King's own hand!

No Medea, no. It's nature. It's natural. A man takes longer to grow old. Men ripen with age ... we wither. We women bloom and then we fade but a man grows more mature and wise. We lose our power ... he gains power. That's the way the world goes!

Oh now I see what you are. You're victims! Oh women ... my friends ... I can see so clearly how man has found the best way to work on you. All for his own good! He's trained you to respect the law but he's made whatever *he* wants become the law! His rules ... his creed! And that's what he teaches to you. He knows that you'll learn the lesson and repeat it and submit to it. And never rebel!

Rebel? Oh careful ... be careful, Medea! Don't persist in offending the King and his law. Appease him. Ask his pardon and then he may allow you to stay in your house.

Stay. Stay! Alone? Alone in my own house like a corpse? No voices, no laughter, no love ... not my husband's, not my children's. No, they've all gone out to celebrate the wedding before they've even buried me. And I ... I'm expected to keep silent now for the good of my children. Blackmail. Infamous blackmail! Aiee! Oh women, women, the bitterness I feel! The darkness. Listen. Listen my friends. A terrible thought has been coming into my heart, my brain. Murder. I must murder my children! They'll call me cruel and evil, a wicked mother ... a woman insane with pride. But better to be remembered as a wild beast than a goat! A goat that you can milk, that you can shear and that you can get rid of whenever you want to. Take it to the market and sell it and it won't even open its mouth to bleat against you. Yes. It's what I must do. I must murder my children.

Oh! Medea's gone out of her mind ... she's raving! This isn't a mother talking, it's a she-devil under a spell! A mad bitch!

No I'm not raving, my sisters. This thought has invaded my mind again and again and every time I've cast it out, pushed it from me! I've bitten my hand and beaten my arm with a stone till it was torn and bleeding to stop myself. To stop my own hand from wounding my little children. How could I spill their honey-sweet blood ... gash their tender flesh with a knife! Flesh that I love, flesh of my flesh.

Oh glory be to all the saints in heaven, Medea's sane again—she's

come to her senses. Light a thousand candles, women. Kneel, friends and send up prayers of thanksgiving that Medea has vanquished these evil, horrible thoughts.

Wait. Be quiet women ... my friend There's no need for these swarms of prayers. I never lost my senses I was never insane. It's true that my first thought was to take my own life ... kill myself. Because I could not bear to be driven out of my own home ... out of this town To be banished from this country even though it is not my country and I am a stranger here. Put on cart and taken away like an infected whore who's covered in sores and scabs. Because I am detested by everyone! Even by you ... women ... my friends. Everyon disowns the woman who's been betrayed, the woman who's full o despair and lamentation ... they want to forget her. You'll see! My own children will forget me as soo as I am out of those gates! Just as if they'd never had a mother. And it will be as if Medea had never been born, never grown up, never been loved ... no never been held a man's arms and touched and enjoyed and possessed. Medea die before she was born! And if it's true that I am dead, already killed ... how can I kill myself? I have to be alive for that and the only life that I have is my children! The only life I can take is theirs. They are my own flesh, my own blood

... my life.

...ee! Help, everyone, hurry! Quickly
... go and get ropes to tie up this
crazed mother, Medea. The devil's
stolen her tongue. It's his evil
words coming out of her.

...ook out! Don't come near me,
women! I'll stick this pitchfork into
anyone who dares to touch me!

...et back! Get away! Run! She's
coming for us. Run! No ... stop.
Here comes her man, Jason. He'll
know how to deal with his woman.
Make way ... let him pass. Calm
yourself, Medea, calm down.
Look—It's your husband. See? It's
Jason! Put down that pitchfork,
Medea. That's right. Thank God ...
she's quietened down.

...son ... how touching and
thoughtful of you to leave your
sweet rose, your bride-to-be just to
come and find me. What a fine
honest face you have as you come
towards me but I can see that
you're agitated. You look
displeased. Don't be alarmed ... it
was all a joke. I was only playing
at being mad. Just to give my dear
friends here a fright and see them
run away screaming. So I could
laugh. Laugh till I pissed myself!
Just playing ... that's all I've got
left to pass the time. But don't be
afraid dear Jason. I'm good now.
I've thought the whole thing over
and now I can see reason. I realise
what a fool I was to think I could
do such a thing. It was only my
own sick, twisted rage ... the

jealousy of a petty woman. I'm
always forgetting that I'm a
foreigner and I should be docile
and happy and well mannered
because people here have been so
kind and loving to me. I can see
now that I got angry like that
simply because I'm a woman and
women are weak. Of course! It's a
woman's nature to give way to
spite and envy and lamentation.
Forgive me, dearest Jason for being
so self-obsessed. It's wonderful that
you've got yourself a new young
wife ... new bed, fresh sheets and
new, much grander, relatives. And
you've got them for me too
because your relatives will be mine
as well and that makes me very
happy. It all makes me happy. If
you'll let me, I'll come to your
wedding. I'll prepare your bed with
lavender-scented sheets and better
than a mother would I'll tell your
young bride the ways of pleasuring
her man. Now are you convinced
that I'm sensible again, Jason?
How could I have called you a
traitor? A man can't be a traitor
just because he exchanges his
woman. The woman should be
happy and contented with being a
mother ... that is her great reward.
What I'd been thinking, you see,
was that it was shameful blackmail
the way your men's law allows you
to exchange us. And I was thinking
that the worst infamy is that you
imprison us women in a cage and
hang children round our necks to
keep us quiet ... the way you hang
a wooden collar on a cow! Then

she's meek and submissive. All the better for you to milk her! All the better for you to mount her! Such silly things I was thinking, Jason ... and I still think them! And I am going to demolish this cage and this infamous yoke and this infamous blackmail. You and your laws have bound me with chains to my own children and forced me to bury myself with my own hands! Oh women, oh my friends ... listen to how I'm breathing. With one breath of mine, one huge breath, I feel as if I could breathe in all the air in the world! My little children have to die, Jason so that your shameful laws can be shattered into pieces! Give me a weapon women, my friends ... put it into my hand And desperate Medea drive, driv the knife into the tender flesh of these children ... the blood ... the sweet blood! Forget, my heart, th these are the children of this flesh ... the blood! ... and don't falter even when they cry out: Mother, have pity! Have pity, Mother! A outside the city gates all the peop will shout: Monster! Bitch! Murderess! Unnatural mother! Whore! *(Softly)* And I will weep and say to myself: Die ... die and let a new woman be born. *(Shouting)* A new woman! A new woman!

End of pl

Accidental Death of an Anarchist

Adapted by Gavin Richards for
Belt & Braces Roadshow Company
from a translation by Gillian Hanna

Accidental Death of an Anarchist is a sharp and hilarious satire
on police corruption in Italy. The play concerns the case of
anarchist railway worker Giovanni Pinelli who, it was claimed,
'fell' to his death from a police headquarters window in 1969.
Pinelli was said to have jumped out—past seven policemen. The
window was wide open—on a freezing midwinter night. He
sustained an injury to the nape of his neck—during his fall. The
fall took place at 23.57 hours or 00.03 hours—depending on
which bit of police testimony is taken. Dario Fo has always put a
premium on entertainment and this play is no exception. On its
first national tour of Italy, it was seen by 300,000 people and
quickly became part of widespread public discussion on the
murder and a major campaign to release other Pinellis from
police custody.

First performed at the Half Moon Theatre, London and later
transferred to the Wyndham Theatre.

'The brothers Marx, Karl and Groucho, have been working in
unison ... when broad farce and social protest miscegenate the
offspring is a real cracker' *Guardian*

Two acts. 6 characters—5 male, 1 female.

ISBN 0 86104 217 4

We Can't Pay? We Won't Pay!
Dario Fo

Translated and adapted by Robert Walker and Bill Colvil

Set in a working class suburb of Milan, this hilarious and
critically acclaimed political farce left-of-centres on a housewives
strike against inflationary supermarket prices and the
politicisation of their stuffy Communist trade union spouses.
Their direct action—looting the shelves—leads to immaculate
conceptions (and many misconceptions), Maoist cops and
Keystone cops, and 'miracles' of all sorts.

First produced at the Half Moon Theatre, London.

Two acts. 8 characters—6 male, 2 female. 5 performers.

ISBN 0 86104 204 2